JEWISH FOLK AND HOLIDAY SONGS

Compiled, arranged and edited by
JOHN W. SCHAUM
for Piano, Organ, or Electronic Keyboard

Text Edited by
CANTOR ROY GARBER
formerly of Congregation Emanu-El B'ne Jeshurun, Milwaukee, Wis.
Transliteration Revised by
ALFRED CAHN and MIRIAM BEN-SHEMUEL

FOREWORD

This collection of Jewish Folk and Holiday Songs has been produced to provide artistic keyboard transcriptions of moderate difficulty so that players of modest technical attainments may successfully perform them. The selections are mainly in Hebrew in either the Ashkenazic or the Sephardic dialect. There are a few songs in Yiddish and English. The vocal ranges of the melodies are in suitable keys for group singing.

Although the songs are divided into different classifications, most of them may be interchanged for other occasions and are not essentially restricted to the one indicated. They are intended to be used for all events in Centers, Camps, Synagogues, Hebrew Schools and all varieties of youth and adult Jewish organizations, clubs or groups.

Credit to Alfred Cahn and Mrs. Nathan Slutzky for editorial suggestions. Mr. Cahn has also revised the musical arrangements on pages 22 and 23.

SCHAUM PUBLICATIONS, INC.

EXCLUSIVELY DISTRIBUTED BY

09-45
CC-10

Contents

Pronunciation Guide

Sound	Example in text	English Equivalent
a	sh<u>a</u>	f<u>a</u>ther
ay	<u>ay</u>n	m<u>i</u>ne
e	n<u>e</u>	h<u>e</u>n
ee	sh<u>ee</u>	f<u>ee</u>l
ey	l<u>ey</u>	l<u>ay</u>
i	{ t<u>i</u>k / l<u>i</u>	w<u>i</u>t / l<u>ee</u>
o	{ l<u>o</u>m / n<u>o</u>	h<u>u</u>m / g<u>o</u>
oo	h<u>oo</u>	r<u>oo</u>m
oy	<u>oy</u>	j<u>oy</u>
u	z<u>u</u>m	r<u>oo</u>m

Consonants are same as in English, except those indicated below:

| ch | <u>ch</u>ad | Ba<u>ch</u> |
| g | <u>g</u>i | <u>g</u>ift |

Note: There is no standardization of the Hebrew transliteration and the Pronunciation Guide is only a general aid.

SUGGESTIONS for USE of CHORDS

For PIANO:	*Right Hand:*	Play treble clef melody as written, or in octaves.
	Left Hand:	Improvise an accompaniment (based on chord symbols). Consult CHORD DICTIONARY on page 24.
For ORGAN:	*Upper Manual:*	Right hand plays melody as written.
	Lower Manual:	Left hand improvises an accompaniment (based on chord symbols).
	Pedal:	Play root of each chord (or alternate tonic and dominant of each chord).
For ELECTRONIC KEYBOARD:		Make the same adjustments as indicated for piano. If keyboard has a "split," play melody to right of split point, accompaniment to left.
For GUITAR:		Improvise an animated strum accompaniment based on the chord symbols.

Hatikvah

Maestoso
Israeli National Anthem
mf
Kol - ohd ba-ley-vav pe - nee - mah   Ne - fesh y'-hoo - dee
hoh - mee - yah,   Ool'-fah-ah-tey miz - rach   kah - dee - mah
Ah - yin le Tzee - yon   tsoh - fee - yah;   Ohd loh av - dah   marcato
tik-vah-tey - nu   Ha -   tik - vah   shnoht ahl - pah - yim,
Lih-yoht ahm chof-shee   be - ahr - tsay-noo   b'eh - retz Tzee-yon vee- roo-shah-lah-yim.

Hevenu Shalom Aleychem

Sabbath Greeting Song

Artza Alinu

Folk Dance

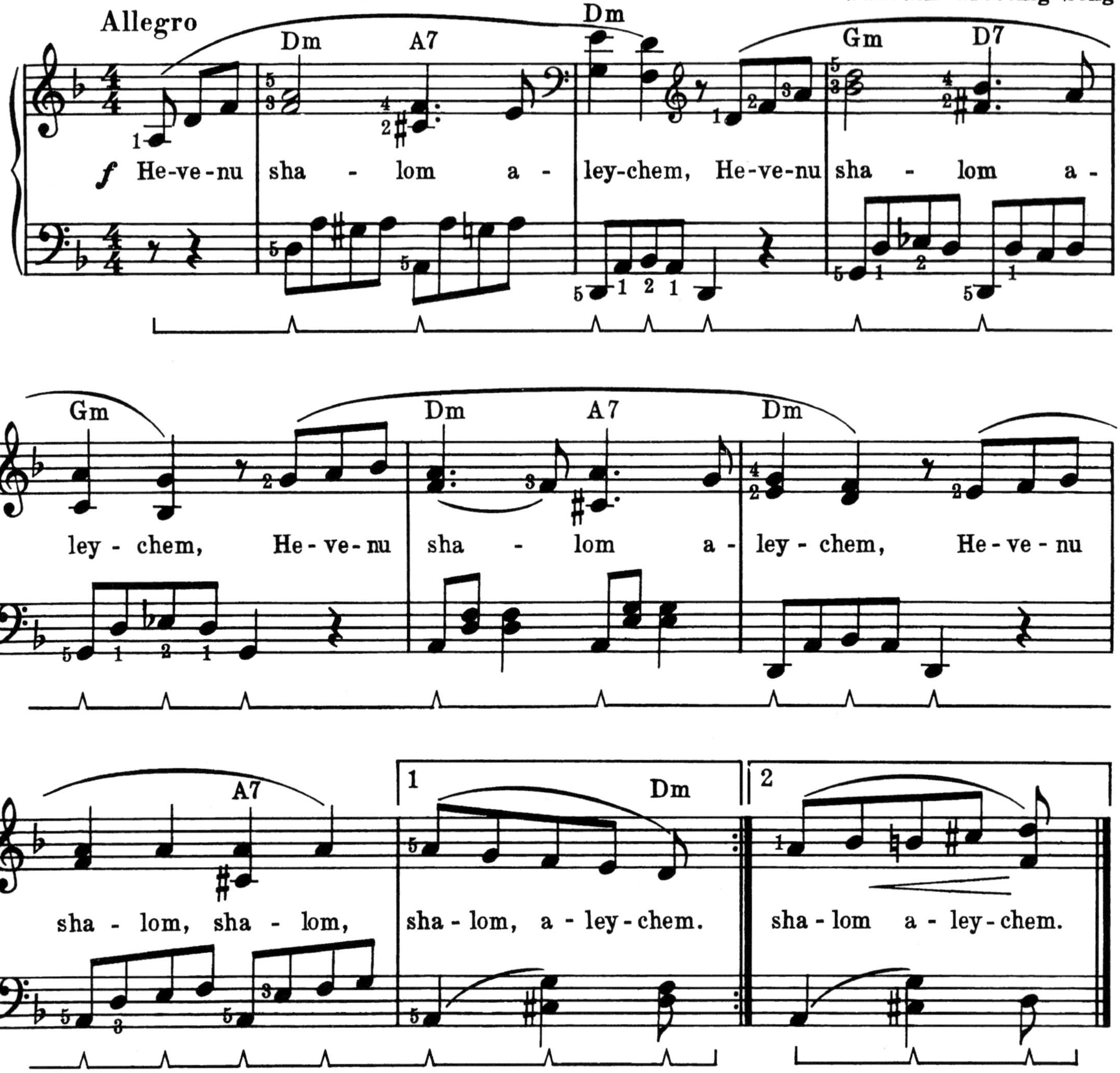

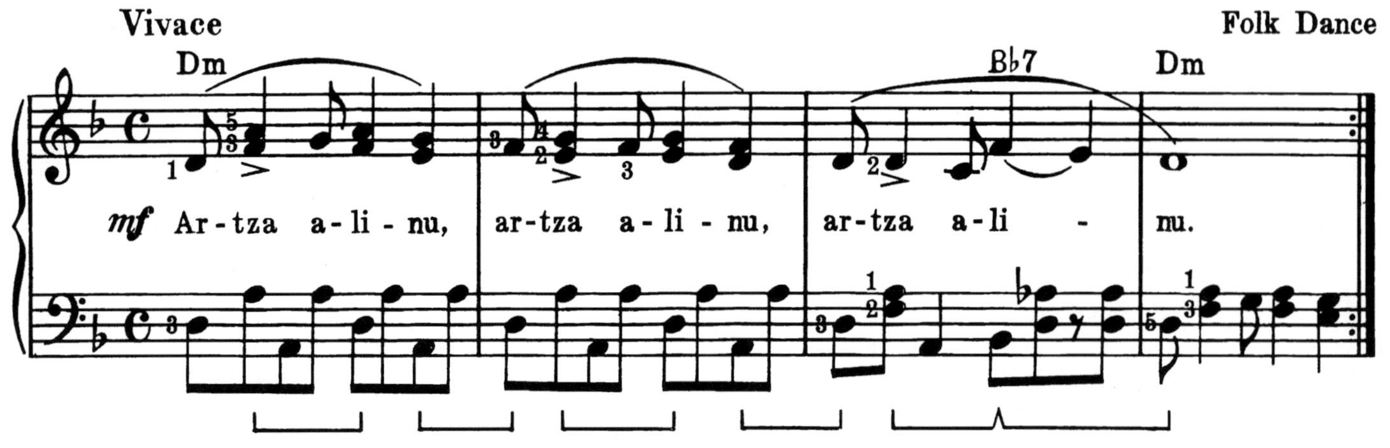

Shalom Chaveyreem*

Animato

Folk Song

*May be sung as a four-part round.

Hava Nagila

Allegro
Israeli Folk Song
E
E7
f Ha - va   na - gi - la, Ha - va   na - gi - la,
Am
Ha - va   na - gi - la v' - nis - m' - cha.
E   Dm   1 E
2 E
cha.   Ha - va n' ra - ne - nah, Ha - va n' - ra - ne - nah,
Dm
Ha - va n' - ra - ne - nah,   v' - nis - m' cha.
E   Dm   1 E   2 E
cha.   cha.
Am
mf U - ru,   U - ru   a - chim,
poco a   poco cresc.

ff U - ru a - chim b' - lev sa - mey - ach, U - ru a - chim b' - lev sa - mey - ach,
Dm
U - ru a - chim b' - lev sa - mey - ach, U - ru a - chim b' - lev sa - mey - ach
E Dm E E7 Am
U - ru a - chim, U - ru a - chim, b'lev sa - mey - ach.
E E7 Am
f Ha - va na - gi - la, Ha - va na - gi - la, Ha - va
1. E Dm E 2. Dm E7 Am
na - gi - la, v' - nis - m' - cha. v' - nis - m' - cha.
8......!

Zum Gali Gali

Lama Suka Zu

Folk Song
Andante
mp
Lama suka zu, Aba tov sheli?
Lama suka zu, Aba tov sheli? Ley-
shev basuka, yakiri, Leyshev basuka, chavivi, Leyshev basuka, yeled cheyn, Yeled cheyn sheli. Leyshev basuka, yeled cheyn, Yeled cheyn sheli.

Eli, Eli

Traditional Yiddish Folk Song

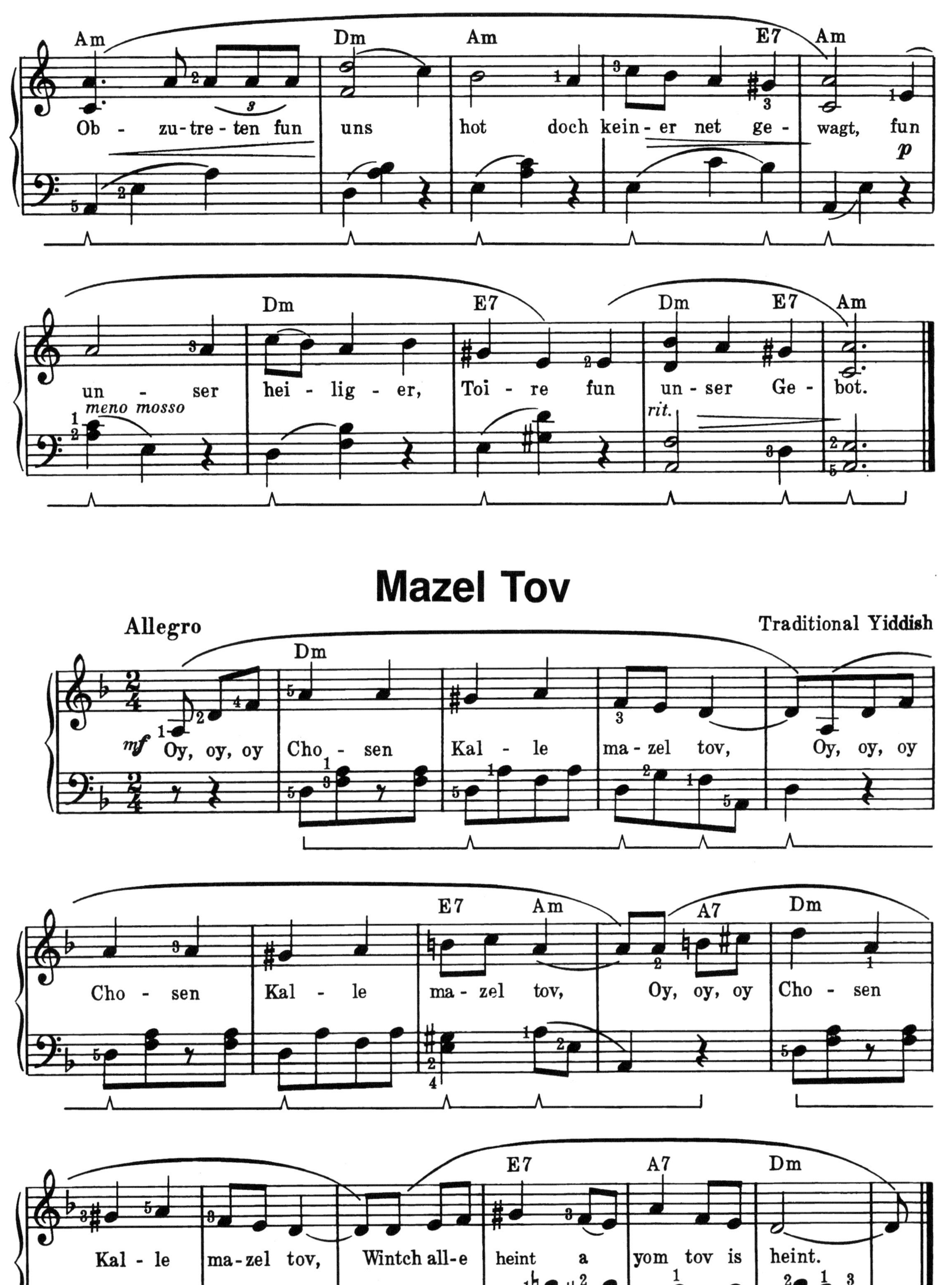

Mazel Tov

Allegro

Traditional Yiddish

Avinu Malkeynu

Kol Nidrey

Traditional
Liturgy
mp Kol nid-rey ve-e-so-rey va-cha-ro-mey ve-ko-no-mey ve-chi-nu-
yey v'-ki-nu-sey u-sh'-vu - os.
mp Kol nid-rey ve-e-so-rey va-cha-ro-mey ve-ko-no-mey ve-chi-nu-
yey v'-ki-nu-sey u-sh'-vu - os.

Rock of Ages

(Mo-oz Tzur)

Chanuka Oy Chanuka

Yiddish Folk Song

Chanuka Song

English Words: E. Fragen

Traditional

Con brio

Purim Day

(Chag Purim)

English Words: E. Fragen

Traditional

Giocoso

Eliyahu Hanavi

Go Down Moses

Chad Gadya

Allegretto
Traditional
Chad gad - ya, Chad gad - ya. De - za - bin a - ba bit - rey zu - zey,
Chad gad - ya, Chad gad - ya. Ve - a - ta shun - ra ve - a - chal le - gad - ye, De-
za - bin a - ba bit - rey zu - zey, Chad gad - ya, Chad gad - ya. Ve-
a - ta kal - ba ve - na - shach le - shun - ra De - a - chal le - gad - ya. De-
za - bin a - ba bit - rey zu - zey, Chad gad - ya, Chad gad - ya.

Boruch Eloheynu

Eyn Keyloheynu

Liturgy

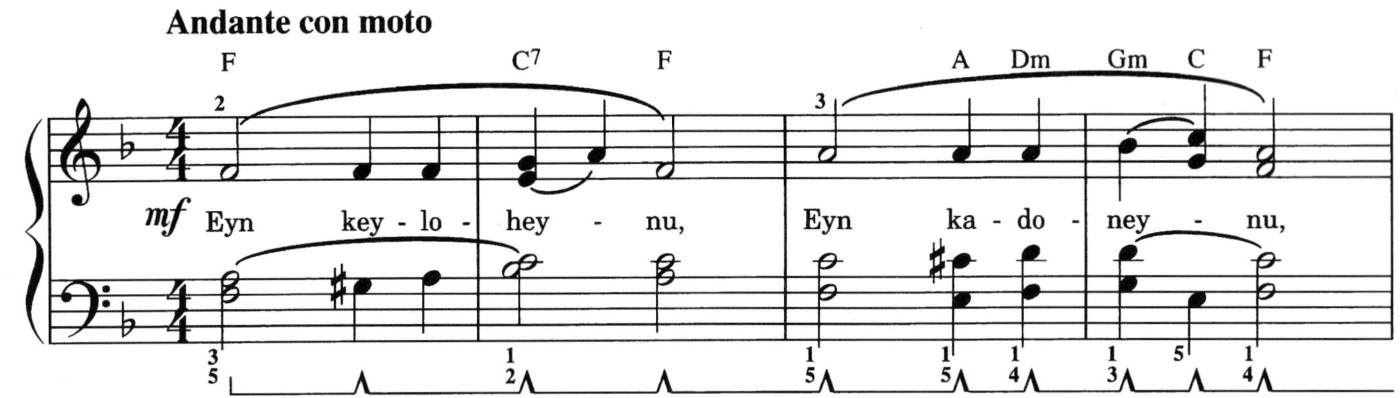

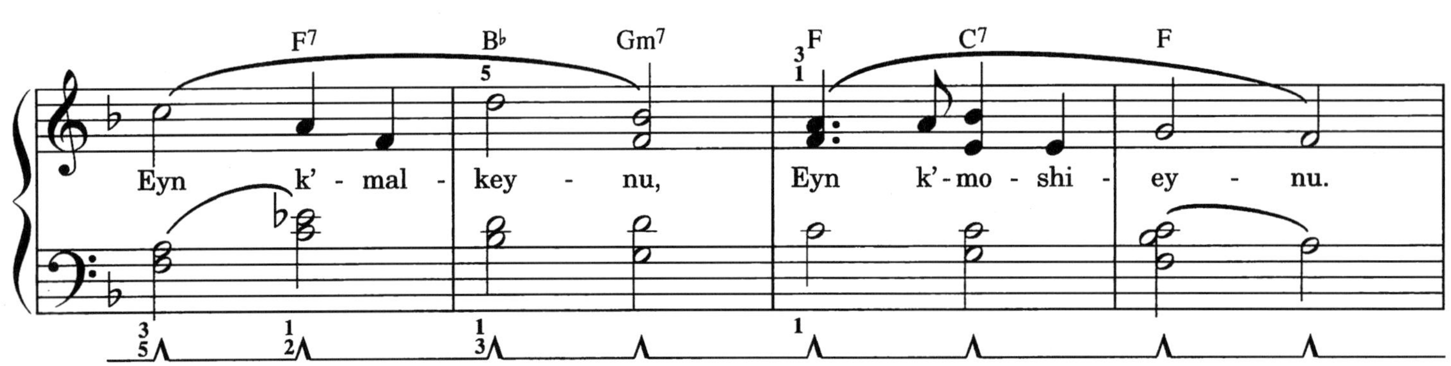

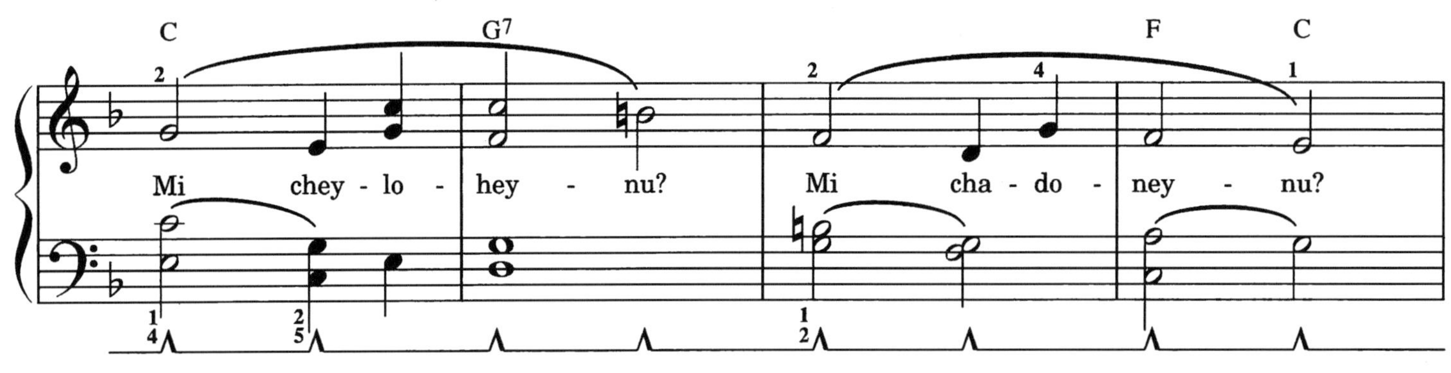

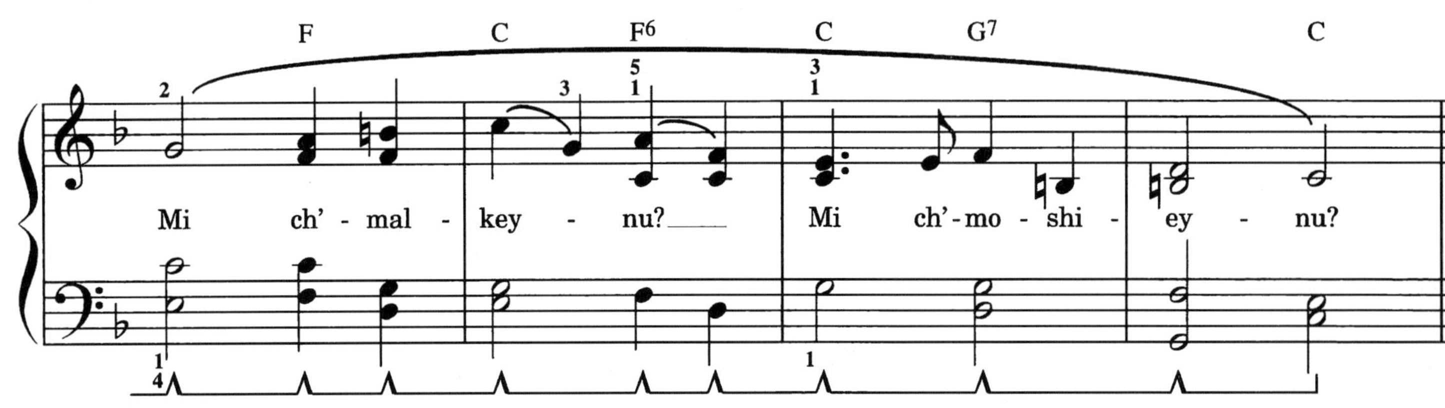

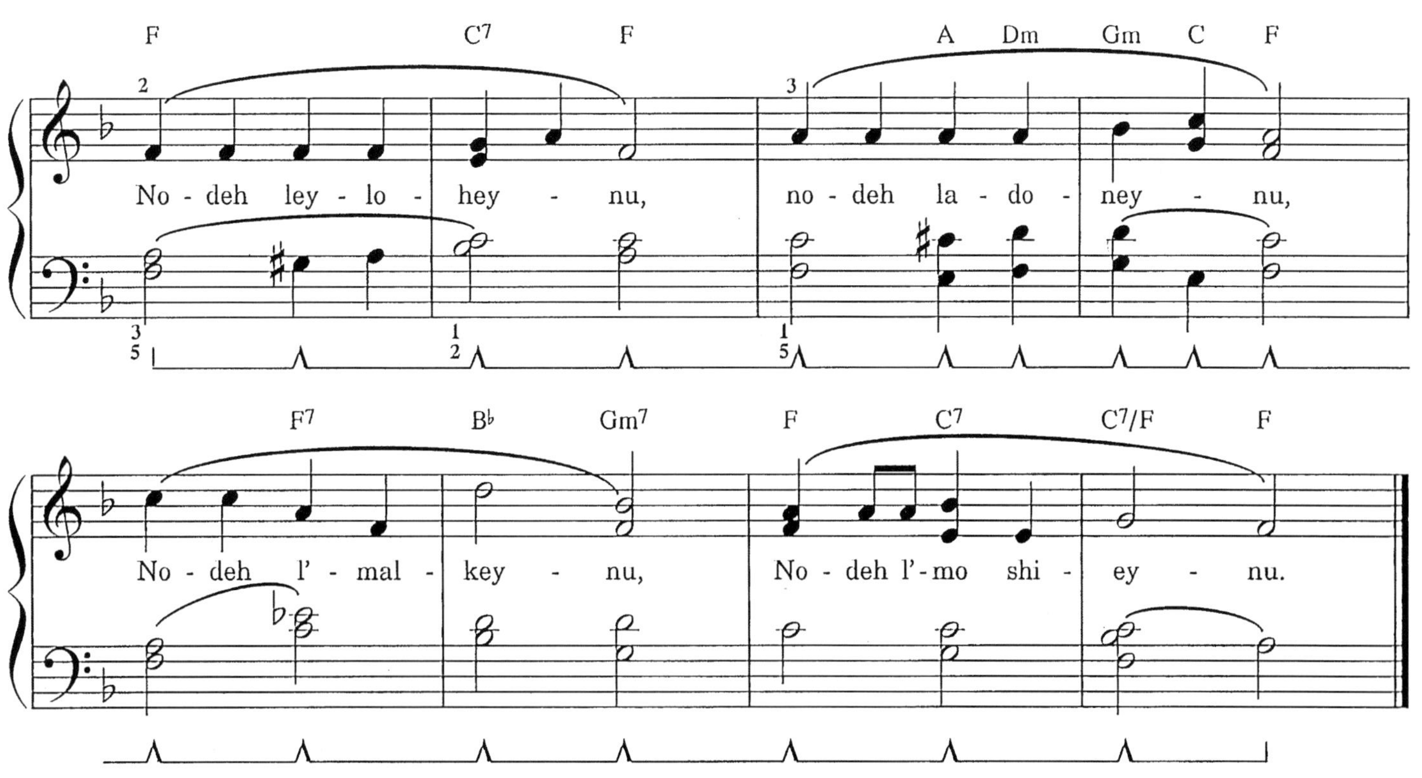

F   C7   F   A Dm Gm C F
No - deh ley - lo - hey - nu, no - deh la - do - ney - nu,
F7   Bb   Gm7   F   C7   C7/F   F
No - deh l' - mal - key - nu, No - deh l' - mo shi - ey - nu.

Adon Olam

Liturgy

Traditional

Andantino
Cm Fm Cm Fm Cm G7 Cm D7
mf
A - don o - lam a - sher ma - lach, B' - te - rem -
Eb Cm Gm D7 Gm G7 Cm
kol y' - tsir - niv - ra, L' - eyt na - a - sa v' -
Eb Bdim Cm Bb Eb Fm Cm G7 Cm
chef - tso kol, A - zai me - lech sh' - mo nik - ra.

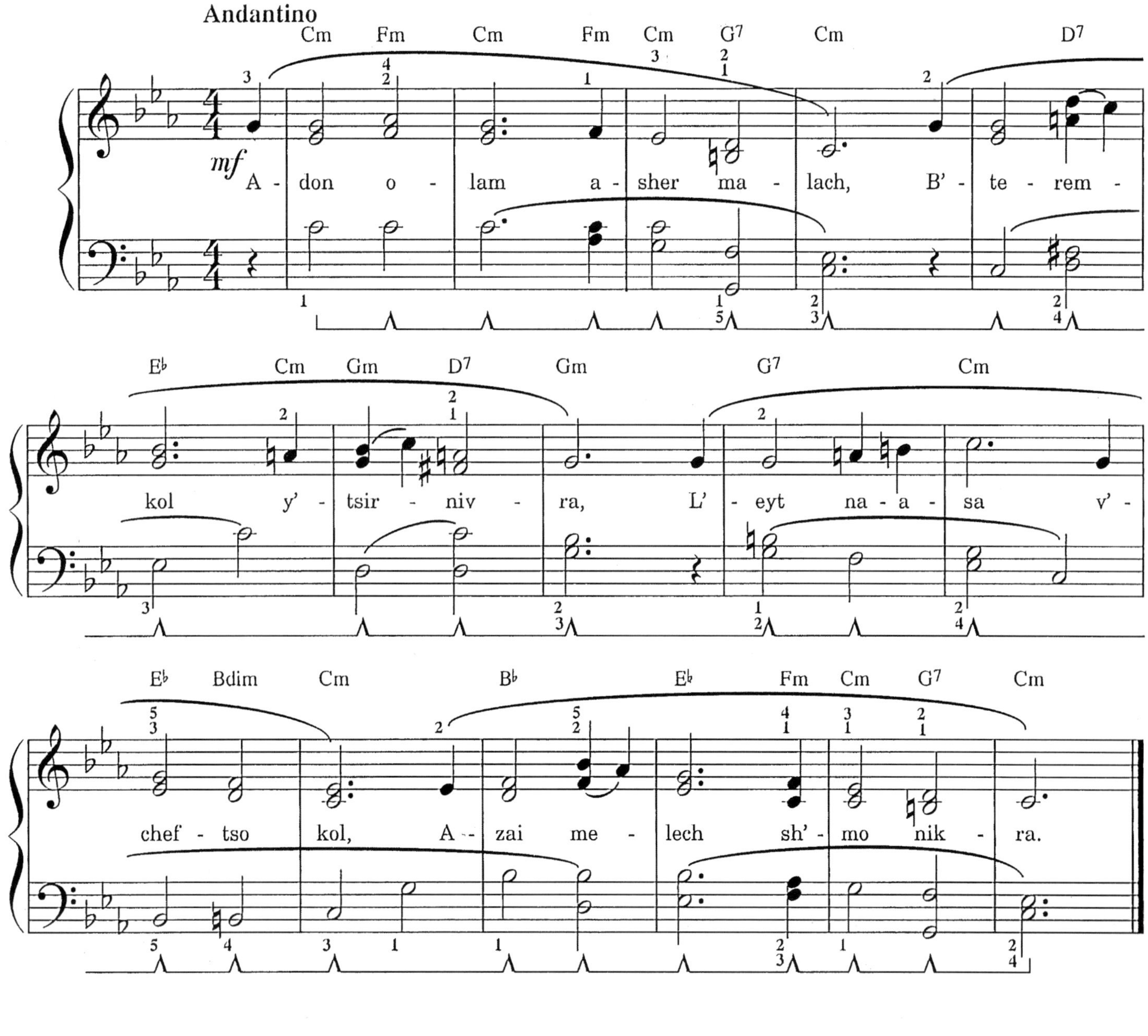

Schaum Chord Dictionary

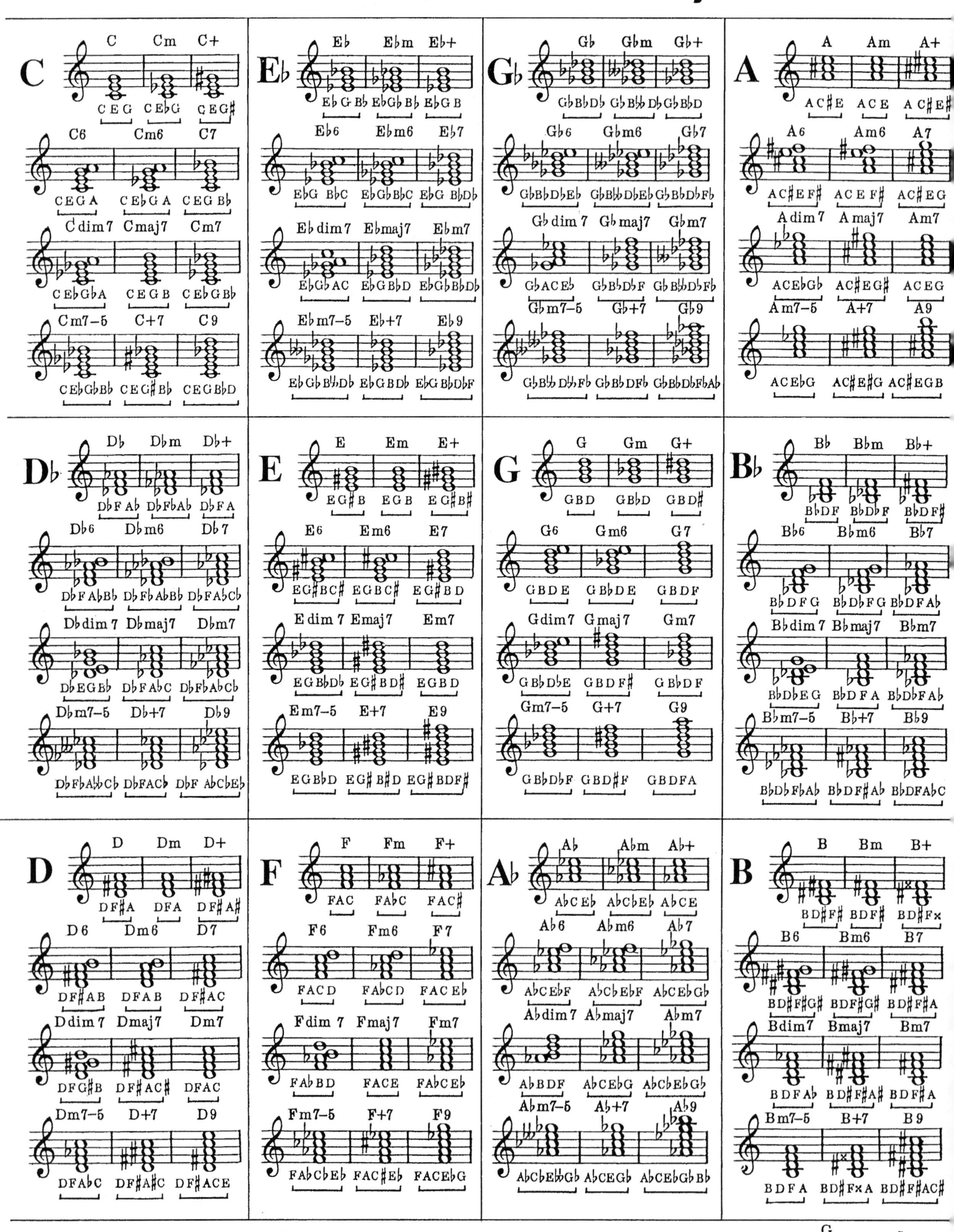